Cool
International Parties

Perfect Party Planning for Kids

Karen Latchana Kenney

A Division of ABDO

ABDO
Publishing Company

visit us at www.abdopublishing.com

Published by ABDO Publishing Company, a division of ABDO, P.O. Box 398166, Minneapolis, Minnesota 55439. Copyright © 2012 by Abdo Consulting Group, Inc. International copyrights reserved in all countries. No part of this book may be reproduced in any form without written permission from the publisher. Checkerboard Library™ is a trademark and logo of ABDO Publishing Company.

Printed in the United States of America, North Mankato, Minnesota
052011
092011

 PRINTED ON RECYCLED PAPER

Interior Design and Production: Colleen Dolphin, Mighty Media, Inc.
Cover Design: Aaron DeYoe
Series Editor: Liz Salzmann
Photo Credits: Colleen Dolphin, Shutterstock

The following manufacturers/names appearing in this book are trademarks:
Elmer's® Glue-All®, Elmer's® 3-D Washable Glitter Paint Pens, Marukan® Rice Vinegar, Roundy's® Soy Sauce, Target® Aluminum Foil, The Original Super Glue® Super Glue

Library of Congress Cataloging-in-Publication Data

Kenney, Karen Latchana.
  Cool international parties : perfect party planning for kids / Karen Latchana Kenney.
      p. cm. -- (Cool parties)
  Includes bibliographical references and index.
  ISBN 978-1-61714-975-7 (alk. paper)
  1. Children's parties--Juvenile literature. 2. Indoor games--Juvenile literature. I. Title.
  GV1205.K46 2012
  793.2'1--dc22
                            2011003498

Contents

It's International Party Time!

Do you know what's cool about international parties? You get to experience different **cultures**! **Research** the country you want to visit at your party. Find **unique** recipes to make. Discover crafts and games to create and play. You will learn a lot about the country. It will also be a blast!

But to make this party happen, you need to plan out the **details**. Start with the basics, like the *when* and *where* of the party. Then move on to details like decorations and **menus**. Create some cool invitations and send them out. And don't forget to plan the activities! They keep the party moving at a fun pace.

Remember to plan and do as much as you can before the party starts. It takes time and hard work to be a host. But it's definitely worth it! Then all that's left for you to do is have fun!

Safety

- Ask for an adult's help when making food for your party.

- Find out where you can make crafts and play games. Do you need to protect a table surface? What should you use?

- Check the party room. Can anything be broken easily? Ask a parent to remove it before the party.

Permission

- Where in the house can you have the party? Are any rooms off-limits?

- How much money can you spend? Where can you shop and who will take you?

- Make sure guests' parents know who will be overseeing the party.

- Can you put up decorations? How?

- How long should the party last? When should guests go home?

- Talk about who will clean up after the party.

Party Planning Basics

Every great party has the same basic **details**. They are the *who, what, when,* and *where* of the party. Your party planning should begin with these basics. Then make lists of everything you need to buy, make, and do for the party. You should also have a list of everyone you invited. Mark whether each guest can come or not.

Who: How many friends do you want to invite? And who will they be? Try to pick friends who will get along and have fun.

What: What is the theme party for? Is it your birthday? Or just for fun? You'll need to explain this on the invitation.

When: Parties are best on the weekends. Pick a Saturday or Sunday. But don't plan the party on a weekend with a holiday.

Where: Is the party at your house, at a park, or at a party room? Explain the details to your guests. And don't forget to include directions!

Favors:

What to buy:

What to make:

Activities:

What to buy:

What to make:

Menu:

Decorations:

What to buy:

What to make:

Music:

Equipment:

Guests:

_____ yes/no

_____ yes/no

_____ yes/no

_____ yes/no

_____ yes/no

_____ yes/no

What's Your Theme?

For international parties, you can pick a country or a continent. That will be your party theme. Once you've chosen a theme, plan all the **details** around it, from the invitations to the games.

Decorate with the country's flag and colors. Or create decorations from one of the country's holidays. **Research** the country and its **culture**. Then use what you learn to make all the elements of your party go together. Check out the party themes on the next page. There are activities in this book to match each one.

Africa

Africa is a continent with more than 50 countries. Two of the African countries are Ghana and Kenya. Beaded jewelry, wooden carvings, and masks are some of the crafts made there.

Australia

Australia is a country, but it is also the smallest continent. It has many **unique** animals, such as the kangaroo and the koala.

India

India is in South Asia. Indian food uses many spices, including turmeric and cardamom. Saris are the **traditional** women's dress.

Italy

Italy is in Europe. It is shaped like a boot. There are many sculptures and paintings by famous artists such as Michelangelo in Italy.

Japan

Japan is in East Asia. It is made up of nearly 7,000 islands. The traditional dress is a kimono. **Origami** is the Japanese art of paper folding.

Mexico

Mexico is just south of the United States. Mexican foods include hot salsa, tortillas, and guacamole.

South America

There are 19 countries on the continent of South America. Many styles of music originated there. Two of the most popular styles are samba and tango.

Don't forget...

After you pick your theme, let guests know all about it. Do they need to bring something or wear special clothes? Let them know on the invitation. That way guests will show up prepared. They'll also be even more excited to party!

Tools & Supplies

Here are some of the things you'll need to do the activities in this book:

egg carton

sugar

rice wine vinegar

soy sauce

baking sheet

aluminum foil

wooden skewers

basting brush

dried beans

honey

saucepan

cutting board

green onions

chicken breasts, boneless and skinless

bottle caps

markers

twine

hole punch

jewel teardrop brads

adhesive business
card magnets

cardboard

tape measure

super glue

modeling clay

card stock

glue

glitter glue

scrapbook paper

duct tape, colored

stickers

paintbrushes

ruler

PVC pipe cutter

PVC pipe

paints

Italiano Invitation

Open this invitation with a pop-up surprise!

What You Need

white card stock, 8½ x 11 inches (22 x 28 cm)

ruler

pencil

scissors

glue

markers

to a party

ITALIANO

When: August 5th, 4:00p.m.
Where: 180 Main St.

Hope to see you there! Ciao!

You're Invited...

Italy Theme

1 Fold the card stock in half crosswise.

2 Lay the card down with the fold at the top. Make marks near the fold 2¾ inches (7 cm) in from each side. Draw a 2-inch (5 cm) line at each mark, starting at the fold. Cut on the lines. Then fold the cut section down and press hard.

3 Unfold the cut section. Then open the card. Push the cut section to the inside of the card. This is the pop-up. Close the card and press it down.

4 Fold another piece of card stock in half crosswise. Glue it over the outside of the first card.

5 Cut a piece of card stock that is 2 x 3 inches (5 x 8 cm). Divide it crosswise into three equal parts. Color the left part green and the right part red. Leave the middle white.

6 Open the card. Glue the flag to the bottom of the pop-up section. Write the party **details** on the card.

More Ideas!

MEXICO THEME
Cinco de Mayo is an important Mexican holiday. Make **festive** invitations with a **sombrero** or **maracas** on them. Use bright colors!

AFRICA THEME
Make invitations stamped with **Adinkra symbols**. Cut Adinkra symbols into craft foam. Press them into ink pads. Then stamp the cards.

JAPAN THEME
Paint a cherry blossom branch on the invitations. Use watercolors to paint a brown stem with pink blossoms.

Pretty Diwali Lanterns

What You Need

ruler

scissors

scrapbook paper in batik print designs

¹⁄₁₆-inch hole punch

jewel teardrop brads

Diwali is the "festival of lights" in India!

India Theme

1 Use a ruler and scissors to cut 15 strips of scrapbook paper. Each strip should be ½ inch (1 cm) wide and 4 inches (10 cm) long.

2 Use the hole punch to make a hole ⅛ inch (.3 cm) from each end of each strip.

3 Put the strips in a pile with the holes lined up. Push a brad through the hole on each end. Spread the ends of the brads open. Press the ends against the bottom of the strips.

4 Now spread the strips apart. Start with the bottom strip. Carefully twist it out. Keep twisting out the strips until they form a ball.

5 Make more lanterns. Place them on tables or hang them from the ceiling.

More Ideas!

ITALY THEME
Italian **cathedrals** have beautiful stained glass windows. You can make your own! Cut a pattern of holes out of a piece of cardboard. Glue colored tissue paper over the holes.

AUSTRALIA THEME
Cut cute kangaroos out of construction paper. Add eyes and other decorations. Then string the kangaroos on a ribbon and hang as a banner.

AFRICA THEME
Make an African safari tablecloth. Use banner paper or a white sheet. Stamp it with elephants, giraffes, lions, and other African animals.

Jumping Joey Magnet

Kangaroo magnets are an awesome favor!

What You Need

paper
ruler
pencil
kangaroo stickers
markers
scissors
adhesive business card magnets

Australia Theme

1. Draw a **grid** of rectangles on the paper. Each rectangle should be 2 x 3½ inches (5 x 9 cm).

2. Put a kangaroo sticker on the left side of each rectangle.

3. Write a message next to each sticker. You could pretend you all just took a trip to Australia! Make one for each of your guests.

4. Use a colored marker to draw a border around each rectangle. Use another color to draw a second border inside the first border.

5. Cut out the rectangles. Stick a business card magnet to the back of each rectangle.

More Ideas!

AFRICA THEME
African beaded bracelets make great party favors. Pick different kinds of wooden beads. String them onto elastic cord.

MEXICO THEME
Fill small bags with Mexican candies and tie with ribbons. Put the bags inside a **piñata**. Everyone takes turns hitting the piñata until the bags fall out.

SOUTH AMERICA THEME
Give each guest a Brazilian Carnival mask. Glue colorful feathers onto plain eye masks. Add glitter and sequins too!

17

What's on the Menu?

A great party isn't complete without delicious snacks and cool drinks! It's best to make finger foods. They are fun to eat and easy to carry. Everyone can still mingle while they snack. To plan your party **menu**, think about a few things first.

Variety

Everyone has different tastes. Make sure you have some sweet and some salty things. Have healthy choices and **vegetarian** dishes too.

Meals

Will your party last a long time? You will need more than one meal if it does. Think about the meals you need to provide. Will your guests need breakfast, lunch, or dinner? And maybe they'll want snacks too.

Amount

How many people are coming? Plan to have enough food to feed everyone.

Time

It takes time to shop for and prepare food. Pick recipes that you have time to make. Remember, there are other things you need to do before the party.

Allergies

Check with your guests to see if they have any food **allergies**. Make sure there are things those guests can eat.

Sample Party Menus

It's fun to plan your menu around your party theme. Here are some examples.

Let's Eat Italian Menu

Smoked Mozzarella and Roasted Pepper Dip

Tomato Bruschetta

Garlicky Meatballs

Gelato Sundaes

Sparkling Blood Orange Juice

Delightful Japanese Menu

Fresh Spring Rolls

Yummy Yakitori*
*recipe on page 22!

Miso Soup

Fortune Cookies

Japanese Green Tea

Tour of South America Menu

Chicken Empanadas

Banana and Pineapple Fruit Salad

Corn Bread

Coconut Flan Dessert

Papaya Juice Punch

Sweet & Spicy Indian Menu

Potato Samosas

Cucumber Spears

Tandoori Chicken Skewers

Cardamom Cookies

Mango-Yogurt Lassi Drink

Ask for help finding easy and delicious recipes to make.

Yummy Yakitori

These sweet chicken skewers are delicious!

What You Need

measuring spoons

4 tablespoons soy sauce

1 teaspoon rice wine vinegar

3 tablespoons sugar

1 tablespoon honey

saucepan

spoon

1 pound chicken breasts, boneless and skinless

cutting board

knife

bowl with lid

baking sheet

aluminum foil

bunch of green onions

8 wooden skewers, soaked in water for ½ hour

basting brush

Theme

1 Put the soy sauce, rice wine vinegar, sugar, and honey in the saucepan. Heat the mixture on the stove while stirring. Continue until the sugar **dissolves**. Take the pan off the heat and let the sauce cool.

2 Cut the chicken into 1-inch (3 cm) cubes. Remember to wash your hands well before and after touching the chicken!

3 Put the chicken and the sauce in a covered bowl. Put it in the refrigerator for a few hours to marinate.

4 Preheat the oven to 400 degrees. Line the baking sheet with aluminum foil. Cut the green onion into 1-inch (3 cm) pieces.

5 Put the chicken and green onion pieces on the skewers. **Alternate** between the chicken and the green onion.

6 Place the skewers on the baking sheet. Bake for 10 minutes. Use the basting brush to brush the skewers with more sauce. Bake for 10 more minutes. Yummy!

Mancala Board Game

This game is played in many African countries!

Africa Theme

1 Cut off the lid of the egg carton. Then cut off the piece that connected the lid to the bottom. Throw that piece away.

2 Cut off the sides of the lid. Stop cutting 2 inches (5 cm) from each end. Then cut the lid in half.

3 Turn the bottom of the egg carton over. Put the halves of the lid over it. The ends of the lid should stick out 2 inches (5 cm) on either side of the bottom. Tape the pieces of lid to the bottom with duct tape. Be sure to cover the holes in the lid.

4 Turn the game board over and paint it. Try painting the egg bowls different colors. Or paint one half one color and the other half another color. Let the paint dry.

5 Look up the rules to mancala on the Internet. Print out the rules so you can teach your friends how to play.

More Ideas!

JAPAN THEME
Japanese fans are pretty and fun to make. Pick a scrapbook paper with an Asian pattern. Cut out two fan shapes. Glue their backs together with the end of a craft stick in the middle.

SOUTH AMERICA THEME
Make **maracas** out of empty yogurt cups. Put in some rice and tape the lids shut. Make a hole in each lid and push a craft stick through each hole. Decorate the maracas with bright colors.

MEXICO THEME
Ponchos are fun to wear. Make one out of a large circle of **fabric**. Cut a hole in the center for your head. Paint **designs** on the poncho with fabric paints.

Clicking Castanets

Make musical instruments used in Mexico!

What You Need

cardboard

ruler

pencil

scissors

super glue

4 bottle caps

markers, glitter glue, and stickers

Mexico Theme

1 Draw two rectangles on cardboard. They should be 4 inches (10 cm) long and 1 inch (3 cm) wide. Make the corners of the rectangles slightly curved.

2 Cut out the rectangles. Then fold each one in half crosswise.

3 Open the rectangles and lay them flat. Put super glue around the edges of a bottle cap. Stick it at one end of a rectangle. Be careful not to touch the glue! Glue another bottle cap to the other end. Glue two bottle caps to the other rectangle in the same way.

4 When the glue is dry, decorate the outsides of the castanets. You could use markers, glitter glue, and stickers. Let the glue dry.

5 Fold the castanets together. Hear the click when the caps meet? Hold one in each hand and click to the beat of the music.

More Ideas!

ITALY THEME
Mosaics are pictures or **designs** made with tiles. Make your own inside a frame. Glue small tiles to the back of a frame. See how **unique** a design you can make!

AUSTRALIA THEME
Make fern paintings called Koru. Look up Koru designs on the Internet. Then use chalk pastels to draw them on paper. Outline the designs in black.

INDIA THEME
Buy a henna kit for your party. You can draw designs on each other's hands. Henna designs are like temporary tattoos. They wash off in a few days.

Perfect Pitch Panpipes

Play these panpipes at your party!

What You Need

½-inch (1 cm) PVC pipe
tape measure
pencil
PVC pipe cutter
modeling clay
colored duct tape
twine
scissors

South America Theme

1. Cut five pieces of PVC pipe. They should be 12 inches (30 cm), 11 inches (28 cm), 10 inches (25 cm), 8 inches (20 cm), and 7 inches (18 cm).

2. Roll five balls of clay about ½ inch (1 cm) across. Press a ball over one end of each pipe. Make sure the clay covers the openings completely. Wrap duct tape around the pipes. Try making each one a different color.

3. Cut two pieces of twine 20 inches (51 cm) long. Tie one of the pieces of twine around the longest pipe. Tie it about 3 inches (8 cm) from the open end. The pipe should be in the middle of the twine. Tie the other piece of twine around the pipe about 3 inches (8 cm) from the first piece of twine.

4. Lay the second longest pipe down with the open end even with the longest pipe's open end. Tie both pieces of twine around the pipe. Tie on the rest of the pipes, from longest to shortest. Make sure the open ends line up. After the fifth pipe, cut off any extra twine.

More Ideas!

JAPAN THEME
Get an **origami** book. Or print origami instructions from the Internet. Pick colorful origami papers. Then have fun folding cool animals.

AUSTRALIA THEME
Make mini-boomerangs. Draw a small boomerang shape on cardboard. Cut it out and decorate it. Bend one end up. Then flick the boomerang off the side of a table.

INDIA THEME
Holi is an Indian holiday also called the Festival of Colors. Get face paints for the party. Take turns painting colorful **designs** on each other's faces.

Conclusion

You ate food from Japan and played games from Africa. Wasn't your international party fun? Your guests tried new things. I bet they learned a lot too. But the party room is a mess! There's still work to do. Make sure you clean up and put everything back in order. Your parents will see what a responsible party host you are.

Was it your birthday? Did you keep track of your gifts? It's important to write down who gave you what. That will make sending thank-you cards easier. Make thank-you cards that match the party's theme. Write something **unique** and personal on each guest's card. It will make your friends feel special. Then send out the cards within a week after the party.

Hosting a party is hard work! There are so many **details** to plan and things to make. In the end, though, it all comes together to make a party to remember. International parties are fun, but what will your next party be? Check out the other books in the *Cool Parties* series for great ideas.

Glossary

Adinkra – symbols from West Africa.

allergy – sickness caused by touching, breathing, or eating certain things.

alternate – to change back and forth from one to the other.

cathedral – a big, important church.

culture – the ideas, traditions, art, and behaviors of a group of people.

design – a decorative pattern or arrangement.

detail – a small part of something.

dissolve – to mix with a liquid so that it becomes part of the liquid.

fabric – woven material or cloth.

festive – cheerful, bright, and exciting.

grid – a pattern with rows of squares, such as a checkerboard.

maraca – an instrument made from a hollow gourd and beans.

menu – a list of things to choose from.

origami – the Japanese art of paper folding.

piñata – container filled with candy, hung up so children can hit it with a stick while blindfolded.

poncho – a rectangular garment with an opening for your head.

research – to find out more about something.

sombrero – a Mexican hat that is tall and has a wide brim.

symbol – an object or picture that stands for or represents something.

traditional – based on customs, practices, or beliefs passed from one generation to the next.

unique – different, unusual, or special.

vegetarian – without any meat.

Web Sites

To learn more about cool parties, visit ABDO Publishing Company on the World Wide Web at **www.abdopublishing.com**. Web sites about cool parties are featured on our book links page. These links are routinely monitored and updated to provide the most current information available.

Index